Read Me if You Need Me

Blue Stallings

BookLeaf Publishing

Presentation by *BookLeaf Publishing*

Web: www.bookleafpub.com

E-mail: info@bookleafpub.com

ISBN: 9789357618533

First edition 2022

For Keela.

You are the thing that found me when I needed it. You have given me words, love, laughter, creativity, curiosity, and all the bright things. I only hope I can return the favor tenfold. I love you, I adore you, I believe in you.

ACKNOWLEDGEMENT

I want to acknowledge the people who got me here, because who are we without the villages who carry us when we cannot stand. If there's anything I've learned about life; it's to love those who love you unabashedly, to say "thank you" more than you say "you're welcome", and to be better than you were yesterday. Here's my attempt at three birds with one stone.

To Serenity Hulsey; for love, for confidence, for friendship in the appropriate regards, for closeness, for many things I can't list here and can never repay. I love you.

To Ms. Renee Hargrove and Ms. Jill Sparks; for belief in my ability to tell a story, for being funny but also real, and for seeing the artist in me before I ever considered the possibility out loud. I say with no small reason, kids need great teachers and amazing role models, and you were both outstanding in those categories. Y'all made me writing this to you one day seem like it could be reality and now here I am.

To my Created Family: Miranda and Wendy Phelps, and Mom (Tera Vanover or Phelps, but always just Mom to me). It's usually true that troubled kids seek out their family, and I am More Than Lucky y'all took me in the way you have. You've given me a mother, sister, a grandmother for my child, a place to live, clothes off your back, food out of your fridge...all in the literal sense. You've protected and loved and supported me to the best of your ability and then some. My life is an acknowledgment to y'all's ability to love.

To Amanda Mayes and Calista Brown specifically. If you don't already know this, you two are The reason I make it through daily life. I wouldn't trade our friendship for a house on a Floridian beach and y'all know what that means. If this relationship we have doesn't last our lives, these words will: I don't tell the two of you how grateful I am for your existences enough. Thank you.

And To Carter Jessup. Thank you endlessly for showing me love still exists in the world, for giving me more to write about than I know what to do with, for always giving me a hug when I ask, for letting me take my time, for building all the things and everything I ask and some I don't, and other things they haven't created words to explain yet. Life with you is fun and exciting and beautiful and crazy and all the things I'd thought I'd lost. I love you, I love you, I love you.

I have no idea where I'd be without all of you, but I know I couldn't and wouldn't be writing this book. And for that, I'm forever and immensely grateful.

PREFACE

Dear Readers,

I want to start by saying I have no credentials to write this book. I went to college for two days, and never furthered my education past high school. My current occupation (although that may change by the time you read this) is Line Cook. What I do have is experience...in life and love, in death and grief, in BPD and Bipolar Disorder and mental illness, in childhood sexual abuse and sexual assault in general. The list goes on but I'll save that for later.
Much of my life has been conducted in dark places, and, looking back, I've realized that maybe my story is more than what I talk about for an hour on Thursdays. Years of therapy brought me back to my childhood love, poetry. My dad once told me, "All the great poets are dead." But I think he missed the point of why I was writing. Why I'm still writing.

But you'll understand, I'm sure. Maybe you deserve to hear it. Maybe you need to hear it. Whatever the reason that brought you here, I'm glad you are.

With love and all the bright things,
Blue

A Letter to my Fourteen Year Old Self

I know you want to die.

I want you to know that through the next five years, the mental health discussion will change. No, they won't stop showing that damned suicide awareness video from 2007 every single year in class and I know you think it's no longer accurate. And although all the teachers will tell you it's better than nothing, I want you to know you've held hands with death longer than they have. They've never been asked if they've thought about hurting themselves except for at the hospital, but they aren't on the same floor you usually are. And you would know because you're up there so much, the nurses know your first name before reading the paperwork.

No, what I mean is that soon enough you will find a website that glorifies what brings you shame. You'll realize you aren't alone, but that you still feel like you are, and despite you not having realized it yet, that sometimes is worse. What they won't tell you is that mental illness isn't always self care posts and affirmation statements. Sometimes, it's missed therapy appointments and drug dependancies. It's real, raw pain that seems to burn your rib cage every time someone touches you as if internal fire would make your skin hotter than stove top burners. It'll drive you into the arms of abusive lovers and the only courage you'll find is in the stories that cover the bruises better than concealer.

What they don't tell you, is the strength you'll find in relapses of all kinds. Sobriety is earned everyday, but there's something powerful in giving up. Being older is harder than people think when you've spent your entire childhood living up to this image of maturity. When most girls your age were partying and living carefree, you picked up boys like it was your oxygen. You don't know who to be when you don't belong to someone and that's not okay. I know that nobody will take the time to tell you that, but he can't help you find your worth hidden somewhere between your legs. And when you come to accept your pansexuality, I want you to know that girls aren't what you've been missing all these years. A person cannot fill that soul-sized hole in your chest, it was made for you.

You'll spend these next few years searching for yourself in other people, avoiding therapy, and self destructing. Your problems are less like an atom bomb and more like termites, a slow agony of hollow support beams and structural defects. I never thought it possible, but empty rooms just feel more vacant with you inside them. And I never believed in ghosts until I saw your eyes in the mirror last night. Despite the addictions and abuse and trauma, there's quite few things in this world that you'll miss out on. Buying your first (legal) pack of cigarettes. Getting your first piercing. Sneaking out too many times to count, with sisters and friends and lovers alike. New cereal flavors and you haven't even tried your favorite food yet. So many concerts that you'll forget and lose count, which honestly is a blessing in itself. Loving people, from afar and sometimes so close that it hurts. Painting walls and owning a car. Getting your drivers license. Impromptu karaoke sessions and shared cigarettes. A glass of wine after a long day. Going to the zoo and museums and still having as much fun at 17 as you did at 7. Your daughter's first smile.

I know you want to die.
I want you to know, I'm happy you stayed.

Love always,
Someone who never would have existed without you

I Am My Own Gardner

My body is a haunted house;
I play guitar outside, in the garden.
It occasionally begins to feel like home;
but the walls, they like to sharpen.

I can't tell which team the ghosts are on,
sometimes they greet me like long lost friends.
At night, they scream until the dawn is breaking.
I guess it just depends.

I spend most of my days outside,
the house reeks of the past.
I admit the garden isn't the prettiest either,
I don't remember if you asked.

It seems as though I'm seeking flowers,
and yet there's none to find.
So I'll sew seeds to the soles of my shoes,
in the garden inside my mind.

Yellow Paint

I've heard
Vincent Van Gogh used to drink
yellow paint
because he thought it would
make him happy.

I drank the nights away with
straight vodka shots,
trying to blink away
the sad artist's eyes
lurking behind my eyelids.

Looking back on these
past few years makes me wonder.
If you could look through my old photos
and find all the times
I was smiling with a mouthful of
the brightest yellow paint.

I Feel like Cinderella, and Not in The Good Way

I've read about relationships
in storybooks since I was little.
Fairytale endings
with weddings to assholes
who never thought to ask
the princess what
her favorite color was.

I don't believe in
love at first sight.
I believe in love at first fight.
When you cry on the
bathroom floor together,
and find that breakage is what binds us
not attraction.

The thing is
when you give someone
your heart,
it is not the leaving
that will break you.
It's the realization
you were the last to know.

Now
when I go to the bathroom,
I hug the cold tiles.
Drag my fingernails until they bleed.
Talk as if you're laying beside me.
I know you never asked,
but my favorite color is purple.

This is a Metaphor for Grooming

to the boy
who thought i was
beautiful and nothing else
i thought that was enough
that if
you saw beauty in me, my
edges would soften into
something more holdable

bloodhounds
run based off scent
i thought i'd memorized
the smell of hurt but with you it hid
behind sickly sweet promises,
dissolving stitches
masquerading as
permanent fixes

how can
i explain the
moment i realized
a bunny was a bear trap
when your jagged teeth crushed
solid bone i thought

bear traps don't
need things to
be more
holdable

they just need
them to hold
still

Why I'm 7-Eleven and You're Getting Gas

I play a part in everyone's story
Though I promise I'm not looking for credit or
glory
I'm merely curious if there's a reason
Why I'm never permanent no matter the season

I'm the neon glow of a 24-hour gas station
The last minute weekend vacation
People proclaim I'm a necessity
I'm left feeling that somehow I owe them this
nicety

My soul is the human equivalent of a drive-thru
Viewed constantly as though I'm here to serve
you
And I know it might read I'm feeling resentful
But it's my promise this poem isn't vengeful

I'm just hoping when it's finally my turn
to live and breathe; to love and learn
You'll learn to be okay with playing your part
and I'll no longer be cast as a shopping cart

There's Something About Repeating Yourself that Makes it More Pathetic

i was a broken record
(please stay, please stay, please stay)
you were past the point of bored
(get away, get away, get away)

in your silence
between my pauses in breath
i didn't notice
you had already left

A "Keeper", Not a Hoarder

That's what I'd call myself. I keep things.
Because I can't keep people.
It started with a red rhino in the back of my
drawer. That became a box.
I keep it there so it doesn't fade or break.
One might go as far as to say it is unlikely that
will happen,
But in a world of what-ifs and you dying
The impossible possibilities seem to become
reality, I vote it stays.
One of my ex boyfriends undid the rubber band,
Opened the box, and called me a hoarder
When I refused to throw it away.
It's trash, he says.
But it is not. It is a green army man, a hospital
bracelet, a Bobby pin, three pennies, a dead
lighter,
a red rhino.
But how could I explain it's actually my
grandmother's kitchen table and the glow of the
overhead light as it hit your face for one of the
last times. It's staying up till midnight and a boy
who loved me so much he saw me in everything.
Even small, plastic, red rhinos.
I've tried to explain why I see love in

Dawn dish soap, and dirty toothbrushes and a
box full of "This reminded me of you"
Instead I find myself keeping receipts, and
Tickets and fortunes and notes,
And all of these memories tucked inside a box,
Guarded by a red rhino in the back of my
drawer.

Consider This My Will & Testament

If I am to go
Before my daughter
Let her sleep inside the garden
Where I used to plant my roses
So that she may rest her head
And be reminded of me

Let her adorn all of my jewelry
The diamonds, silver and gold
Wrap herself inside my bed sheets
And cry as many times as she needs
So that I may come as close to holding her
As I ever will again

May she dance in the halls
Of her childhood home
Getting rid of all the clutter
So that there will be enough room
For her laughter
And I'll never forget the sound

When I'm supposed to go, before my daughter
I'll kindly refuse
I'll brush her hair with the breeze instead

Wipe her tears with warm sunshine
And when she's finally ready,
We will go together

Counting Stars and Why I Love You Still

I have a thought of you for every star in the sky.
Sometimes I like to lay outside, alone, and list
them to myself.
Just in case, I don't whisper. You're not
eavesdropping; you're missed.

One. You made me hate eye contact.
Two. You saved my favorite shoes.
Three. You loved art, maybe more than me.
Four. I'll finally admit it, you were a good
kisser.
Five. You were a lightweight when it came to
drinking and I wish you would have just
stopped.
Six. You had the prettiest smile. I should have
realized when it went away.
Seven. You spent most of our relationship trying
to teach me something I didn't understand. It
was always just out of my grasp, but I wasn't
stupid. I was young.
Eight. I don't know why but I associate you with
butterflies. I see them everywhere now, and I tell
myself it's you but I wish I could know for sure.

Nine. I never told you, but I think you were the
only person I ever truly let know me. In some
ways, I feel like you're the only person who ever
will.
Ten. I remember what our last fight was about,
and you were right about some things. I'm sorry.
I didn't know how to say it then, and I waited
too long. I was drunk and hurting and so were
you. Eleven. Do you ever just want to take back
your words? I said the wrong thing. Twelve.
Someone said, missing you comes in waves; this
is a tsunami. Thirteen. Do you remember the
night we walked home in the snow? Winter in
Kentucky still sucks.
Fourteen. Fifteen. Sixteen. Seventeen.

Eighteen. For your nineteenth birthday, we
drove to Nashville with my brother. It was
unseasonably warm, so naturally we all went out
for ice cream in mid-November. Someone made
a comment about never having been in a food
fight, and that's all you needed to commence
nothing less of a battle in the middle of
downtown. We drove home for two hours with
pistachio ice cream in our hair and rosy cheeks.
You'll never be older than this.
Nineteen. I've always wondered what you
wished for blowing out a candle in your ice
cream cone. Or if you have any regrets. It wasn't

my birthday but I wished you were happy. I still
send you Facebook messages hoping you'll
respond as if your ghost could write me back.
And I lay in the yard, talking to dead stars and
stray cats.

Twenty. But just in case, I don't whisper. I don't
want you to think you're only missed in past
tense, you're loved in the present too.

My Therapist Calls This Religious Trauma

i remember the first time i grappled with my
mortality
and, quite honestly, everyone else's too
my family were "good" Christians
the Church-going kind
Sunday Service, youth group wednesday
it wasn't before long
a pastor told me my pigtails would burn in the
fires of hell
if i ever thought to question God
that The Lord made the little boys and girls
to be quiet
i guess it's a good thing i shaved my head
or maybe that pastor lied
so, God,
why do churches try to teach children
the only way to being a good person
is being afraid to die

Drunk Dialing My Ex in 2015

It's been almost a year since you last messaged me, and
less than two minutes since I've wished you would.
I know calling you is self destructive,
but sometimes I think I should.
And the sunflowers you planted to suffocate,
now hold me
In a way you never could.

I'm Filing a Missing Persons Report on My Dead Boyfriend

I searched for you
In every empty parking lot
Every ledge that led to nowhere
All the long stretches of highways
And songs with words
That once meant something

I cried for you
Laying on the bathroom floor
I screamed until my lungs burned
The neighbors called the cops
I told them everything was fine
Because broken hearts are not emergencies

I wrote this for you
Somewhere in the long nights
My walls told me the words
And now that my mind is quiet
I still cannot hear you and
The silence is deafening

You Ate My Childhood Fears for Breakfast

I've always been afraid of monsters
The kind that hide under the bed
Inside the closet
In the dark of the hallway
Even through my adult years
I've followed the rules that keep them at bay
Check under the bed
Shut the doors
Keep a light on, just in case
Upon losing you, I learned
There are things I fear more than monsters
And rules were made to be broken
At least, that's what I tell myself
When I fall asleep leaving my
Bedroom door wide open
And a wish that you'll come home.
The hall light will be on,
just in case.

I Fucking Hate House Parties

Another New Years in New York.
You've been gone awhile now and I'm feeling
funny.
Another champagne bottle cork
Hits the floor outside-a waste of money.

I've somehow never felt more alone.
All of these people are suffocating.
And the bathtub kinda feels like home...
here's your invitation, I'm just waiting.

I don't know if you're reaching out for me.
But in a way, I do.
Cause I'm here running on empty
and I haven't run into you.

So next year, I will watch the ball drop
In Times Square, nonetheless.
I won't be waiting here, I promise.
You wouldn't care about the rest.

Houdini Ain't Got Shit on Me

I'm begrudgingly known as the girl
Who plays with knives or runs with scissors.
To disappear is to gain worth.
My vanishing act has surely gotten quite old,
And my feet are both tired from running.
But neither are quite as tired as my brain of
The same looping thoughts,
Crashing incessantly between my ears;
They drive each heel into the pavement.
I should clarify, the burns were accidental.
We all know the dangers of playing with fire.
But against my better judgment,
and a magician's rule of thumb,
I'll reveal to you this secret.
I tricked myself into believing
every heartbreak
was love.

An Ode to I-75 South at Midnight

There's something about you when you're
empty
You're the perfect companion for nights of little
sleep
The quietest place for the loudest thoughts
Losing pieces of myself to the open window
Finding myself inside the ocean breeze
I never realized why I didn't know home until
I visited the sea
I thank you for always accompanying me as the
girl under the water waves goodbye
I'd like to think you're my soulmate from a past
life
A likeness we share, a special aloneness split in
two
I miss you when we aren't together
When your silence isn't shaped like a hug
I miss me when I'm not going somewhere
Finally okay with just existing
No bigger than a bug

For Lack of Better Poems

I burn myself more than I'd like to admit.
I'm only clumsy when it comes to taking care of
myself,
never self aware enough to prevent calamity.
All the while, others become cracked plates,
the kind you worry you'll shatter just trying to
wash the dishes.
What kind of irony is it, the heartbreakingly
human type, that we can do more damage in the
attempt to care, so much so, to the point of
irrepair.
"I'm sorry"s do no more for people than they do
for plates.
But still, for lack of better words, I say sorry
to those who love me, and to me who burns me,
and to the plate.
And in some ode to human nature and cycles
and the self awareness I lack,
I burn myself. I wash the dishes.
I hurt those I love. I break the plate.
I write the poem where I tell you it would be
redundant to tell you I'm sorry,
But I don't know what else to say.

A Conversation with My Inner Child

If you asked me what is a life well spent
I'd ask you to take a hard look at ours
You'd have to be the judge of that
I'm too grateful, too biased, too kind

I've read we're greater than the sum of our parts
But even reduced to that, I'm honored
You see, I would've traded a thousand lives
For one day starting with your sleepy grin
That one I never thought I'd see again

Our child's laughter, a goodwill trip,
Late night huddles at our house,
Each little moment we'd miss
So honestly I'd say we got a bargain
Paying one lifetime for all of this

In This House

We bake bread on Sundays
and the flowers never die.
This is where laughter and
warm chocolate chip cookies reside.
In fact,
these are considered medicinal supplies.
And a rainy day always has a book;
your jacket, a hook.
In my house, the candles always burn,
not a heart yearns
for a friend,
for a face,
for a warm, familiar place.

If This is My Success Story,
I'm Okay with That

I wrote this book because I had to.
Because you, the reader, needed it.
Because words have a power all their own
And these were screaming to be devoured.
Threatening to crack me wide open
if I couldn't find them a home.
I've searched tirelessly to find a place that felt
soft enough, safe enough,
I lost a few along the way.
Stuck in places they didn't fit,
Left behind for people who wanted to keep them
more than they did me.
Yet the rest were becoming too heavy to carry,
so I built them one instead.
I told them to wait,
That the person I wrote them for
Is surely on the way by now.
I promised there would be enough room
For all of us to stay together this time,
I'm so happy you're finally here.